WATCH THIS!
The Definitive Reference Guide to Video Marketing

By David Spark

Copyright © 2018 Spark Media Solutions

Print ISBN: 978-0-9968602-5-3

David Spark (@dspark) is the founder and president of Spark Media Solutions, a B2B content marketing agency for the tech industry.

Spark blogs at Spark Minute, and hosts the Tear Down Show and the CISO/Security Vendor Relationship Podcast.

For more information about video opportunities, production, or to book David Spark for interviews and speaking engagements, please contact info@sparkmediasolutions.com.

Cover design, illustrations, and book layout by Joy Powers (@joypowers).

SparkMediaSolutions.com

Original printing

WATCH THIS!

The Definitive Reference Guide
to Video Marketing

by

DAVID SPARK

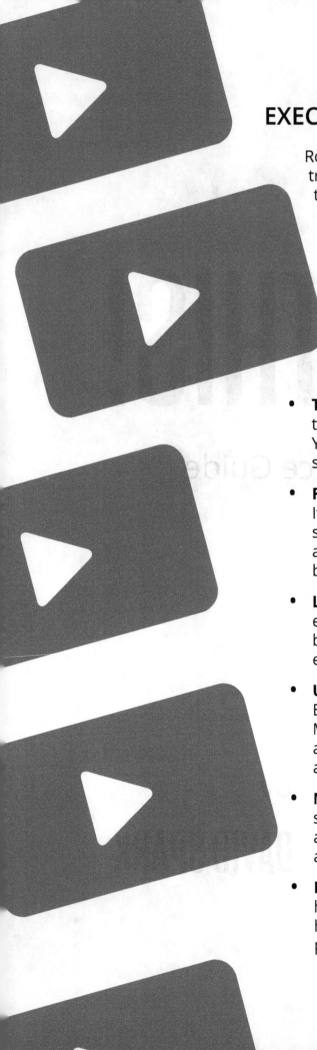

EXECUTIVE SUMMARY

Roughly a quarter of search and content consumption traffic is focused on video. While companies know they need to produce video, they're still struggling to maintain a presence. It's complicated, it takes unique skills, and it can be very costly to sustain an active branded video channel. Some become paralyzed as to what to do next, as they don't even know what they're up against. This ebook simplifies the online video process by breaking down each element and shows how it contributes to capturing your target audience. Here are the top findings from our research.

- **The invisibility trap.** Companies that have poor to non-existent video presences can't be seen on YouTube. That means they're simply invisible to the second most trafficked site on the Internet.[1]

- **Funding not commensurate with online trends.** It doesn't appear B2B tech companies are keeping in step. Given trends in search, social, and traffic, about a quarter of a company's search and social marketing budget should be spent on video.

- **Loose to non-existent branding.** Video branding efforts are frightfully not in line with corporate branding. We were shocked to find this happening even with the biggest Fortune 500 tech companies.

- **Usual suspects.** With few notable exceptions, most B2B tech companies have limited creativity with video. Most of their video content fits expected molds such as customer testimonials, presentation videos, and animated explainer videos.

- **Mostly one-off production.** B2B tech companies are struggling to commit to ongoing video efforts, which are critical for building audience and community around their content.

- **Easy opportunities missed.** Online video has its low-hanging fruit, which are simple opportunities that can have a big impact. Some of the easiest and necessary production options were missed, almost universally.

- ***Online* video introduces new complications.** The sheer number of variables needed to manage online video is daunting. Being successful with online video requires the constant juggling and management of dozens of disparate variables. Quality video production is only one of those variables.

AVOID THE INVISIBILITY TRAP

To be visible on Google, the most trafficked website, you need a website. Almost all companies have a brand-consistent website.

But to appear on YouTube you have to produce videos. That's not nearly as easy. Nor is it critical to starting a business.

But when a company fails to produce brand-appropriate videos, they're making a conscious choice to be invisible to the second-most trafficked website on the Internet.[2]

Let that sink in for a second.

Companies have enormous marketing budgets for search engine optimization, search engine marketing, and content marketing. It's all designed to target people who are proactively searching for information. By not investing in video, the money spent in search and social media marketing simply doesn't reflect where people are searching and consuming content.

- YouTube accounts for 28 percent of total searches on Google.[3]
- YouTube has 25 percent of the market share of social networks.[4]

If you're just measuring eyeballs and focusing on Google search, *your company should be spending about one-quarter of their search and social marketing budget on video marketing.*

FALLING SHORT ON VIDEO GIVES YOUR COMPETITION AN ADVANTAGE

If your company chooses not to be on YouTube, not only are you invisible to this audience, your competitors are at a great advantage to be visible with no challenge from your business.

Relative to text-based media, video is an uncrowded space and proven to be a more attractive option.

Video drives consumption preference, inbound traffic, improved search results, and more time spent on page.

- Four times as many consumers would rather watch a video about a product than read about it.[5]

- When video and text are on the same page, 72 percent of visitors would rather watch the video to learn about a product or service.[6]

- Blog posts that have video attract three times as many inbound links as blog posts without video.[7] The increase in inbound links probably speaks to why having a video on a landing page makes it 53 percent more likely to show up the first page of search.[8]

- A landing page that has a video leads to dramatically more time spent on the page. As compared to pages that don't have video, one study showed an increase in 25 percent more time[9] and another showed 2.6 times more time spent on the page.[10]

VIDEO CONVERTS

Lastly, in my effort to try to convince you to spend a significant portion of your marketing budget on video, here is some data on conversions:

- Companies that use videos in their marketing experience 27 percent higher click-through-rates (CTRs) and 34 percent higher web conversion rates than those that don't.[11]

- Videos that appear in search results have a 41 percent higher clickthrough rate than plain-text results.[12]

- Companies that use videos in their marketing grow revenue 49 percent faster year-on-year than those that don't.[13]

OK, I GET IT, USE VIDEO, BUT...

Even though search, consumption, and conversion trends favor online video, B2B tech companies' entry into video is often viewed as experimentation rather than a competitive tool that must be mastered in order to succeed. This is evidenced by the high number of "one-off" videos and video series that die off only after a handful of episodes. When anticipations run high and immediate return on investment (ROI) falls short, frustration sinks in, with little desire to throw more money at what is seen as a failure.

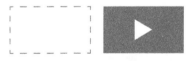

An organization that has no brand in video can't assume they're going to instantly build a video media brand with just one or even a handful of videos. It's literally never happened in the history of media, yet the expectation always looms and it's unrealistic.

It's disturbing to see how some of the largest tech companies, often in the Fortune 500, look to YouTube as a dumping ground for whatever random video they happen to produce. The videos don't appear to be made for an audience yet are delivering on a corporate marketing need, such as presentation videos and customer testimonials.

A YouTube presence is an enormous opportunity to build an ongoing relationship with an interested and subscribing audience. This can be far more powerful than an email list because it's about personal engagement. It's similar to the relationship that can be made with a podcast audience. We believe it's even more powerful because a YouTube presence delivers the audience, algorithm, email marketing, and traffic of YouTube, the second most trafficked website on the Internet.

HELP IS ON THE WAY... JUST KEEP READING

Beyond just the complications of video production, there are a seemingly endless number of variables to manage the publishing and promotion of online video.

In addition to the video tips and opportunities, I provided some context as to what the competition is doing. We conducted research into how B2B tech companies are utilizing video. I wanted to show that this space is still wide open for everyone. Even Fortune 500 tech companies that have enormous budgets are falling short. We didn't see one example of any one company doing everything right.

Tech companies that have little-to-no video presence were not considered in our analysis.

There are multiple video platforms. We looked at the ones we believe have the greatest impact for B2B tech companies.

FORMAT FOR THIS GUIDE

This guide and the ensuing research is focused into two parts.

The first section of this guide is focused on producing and maintaining a YouTube presence. While there are many ways to post videos on the Internet, we have put a significant focus on YouTube since the platform has 78.8 percent of the market share in video.[14]

The second section touches a little on video production issues, plus posting videos to Facebook, LinkedIn, and using platforms that give you more information as to who is watching the content.

Each tip begins with a basic description, and then the following format elements:

OPPORTUNITY

How and why you want to take advantage of this feature to present or market your videos.

DESIGN CONSIDERATIONS

Since there is far from a "one size fits all" methodology, I address various elements to consider when trying to take advantage of this opportunity.

CURRENT TRENDS

We contained our analysis to 50 B2B tech companies across almost all 56 variables. In this section we provide details as to how tech companies are or are not taking advantage of this specific opportunity.

DIFFICULTY AND IMPACT

These opportunities vary dramatically in terms of how complicated they are to pull off and their overall effect once implemented. I created a subjective 1 to 5 scale of *difficulty* and *impact*. Ideally, you'll first want to focus on the items that are the least complicated to pull off (low *difficulty* score) and yet provide the greatest return (high *impact* score).

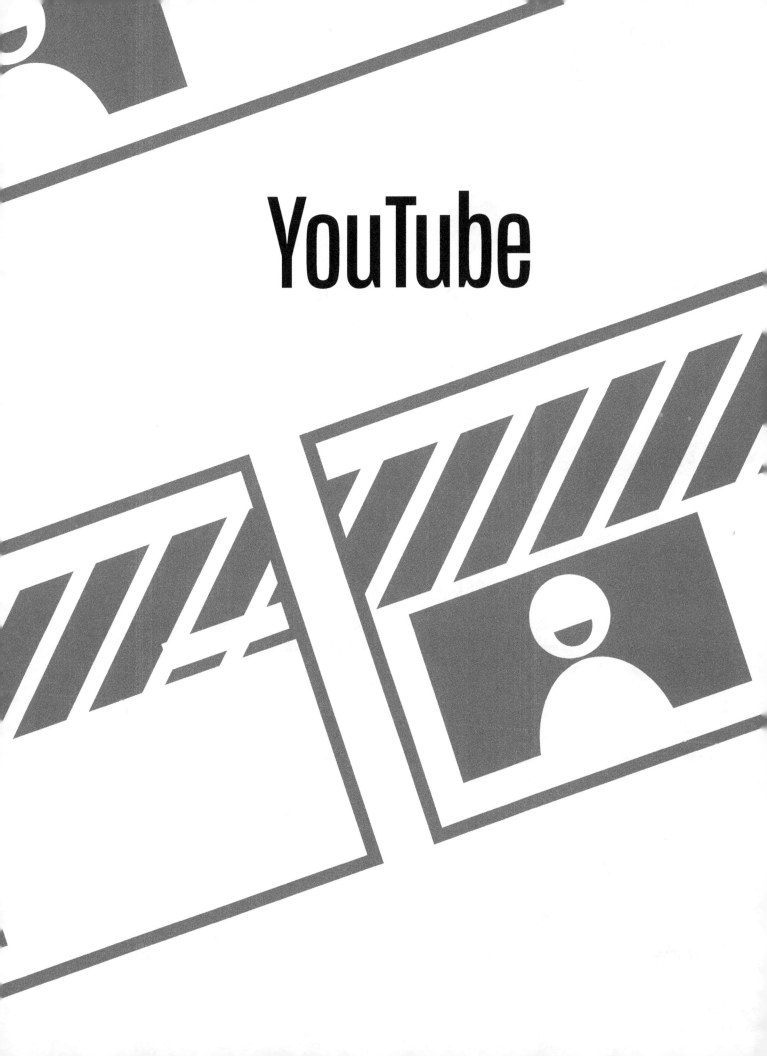

YouTube

1

CREATE BANNER THAT EXPLAINS/INVITES

It's impossible to ignore a YouTube banner. It's big and at the top of the page. Your banner introduces and welcomes visitors to your YouTube page. This single image should answer a visitor's most basic questions:

- Where did I just land?
- Is this YouTube channel for me?
- Should I venture further?

OPPORTUNITY

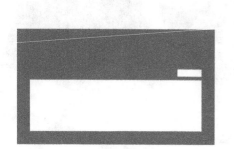

The banner image is an enormous communications OPPORTUNITYto explain what the channel is about, what the users can expect if they subscribe to this channel, and if possible, how often the videos will be published.

DESIGN CONSIDERATIONS

- Don't just add the company logo or tag line in the banner, as it probably won't communicate the content and value of the YouTube channel.

- Make it clear what the channel is about and the value proposition for subscribing.

- Depending on the browser you're using, your logo may appear in the banner (Internet Explorer) or right below the banner (Chrome, Firefox). Plan your design accordingly.

- If you're producing a regular series with the same people in the videos, include photos of those people.

- If you can commit to a regular publishing schedule, make it clear in the banner how often your videos are published (e.g., "New videos every Tuesday").

CURRENT TREND

More than one-third of corporate B2B tech channels provide zero explanation in their banner as to what content their YouTube page offers.

This lack of explanation probably stems from the fact that most B2B YouTube pages have little-to-zero consistent content direction.

Difficulty: ▮▮▮▮▮▮▯▯▯▯▯▯

Impact: ▮▮▮▮▮▮▮▮▮▮▮▮

PROMOTE NEW NEWS IN THE YOUTUBE BANNER

To get the most eyeballs and traffic, news sites put their latest and most valuable news right at the very top of the page. Hey, whaddya know, that's exactly where your YouTube banner is.

OPPORTUNITY

Your YouTube banner does not need to stay static. It's perfectly positioned to announce news, events, new products, live streams, or even specific videos you want visitors to check out.

Assuming you're announcing news on the company website, you should also announce it within your YouTube banner as well, especially if it's relevant and you have a video.

DESIGN CONSIDERATIONS

- Architect a standard design with a designated space promoting the latest information. Don't overload the visitor with information. What's the bare minimum of words and imagery that will direct them where you'd like them to go?

- Update the banner. Don't leave a banner up promoting an event that's passed.

CURRENT TREND

In our analysis, we only saw one company (Infosys) take advantage of delivering new news via the YouTube banner.

Difficulty:

Impact:

3

WELCOMING VIDEO FOR NEW VISITORS

YouTube has a commonly used feature that allows a channel manager to specify which video will autoplay the moment a new visitor or anyone who has yet to subscribe arrives at your YouTube page. Very few companies take advantage of this gigantic opportunity to connect with a new and curious audience.

On blogs and websites, publishers shy away from posting autoplay videos (especially with sound on) because the general consensus is they're annoying. At the time of writing this report, Facebook periodically adds sound to its autoplay videos to the consternation of most everyone.

Where's that sound coming from?

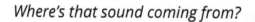

It's the first response when you hear a video start playing that you didn't initiate. The moment we hear them, we're immediately trying to figure how to turn them off because the video appears in a different place.

Conversely, it appears that since its inception YouTube has trained users to assume the featured video will autoplay when they visit anyone's YouTube page. Unlike the appearance of autoplay videos elsewhere on the web, on YouTube it's actually not annoying. It's expected.

OPPORTUNITY

This opportunity rivals the messaging on the banner as the most important first step a company can do to improve the value of their YouTube page.

DESIGN CONSIDERATIONS

- Answer the question, "Why am I spending any time on your YouTube page?"

- What do you think a visitor would like to hear when landing on your YouTube page?

CURRENT TREND

Almost universally, companies presented either a well-produced advertisement or explainer video as their featured video. We saw no examples of videos welcome people to the company's YouTube channel, explaining what they're going to see, and enticing them to subscribe.

Six percent of the companies we looked at didn't even bother changing the settings on YouTube to automatically play a featured video.

Difficulty: �███████████████████▯▯▯

Impact: ███████████████████████

4

CAPTURE ATTENTION WITH FIRST WORDS HEARD VISITING YOUR PAGE

As mentioned previously, an autoplay video with sound is expected on a YouTube channel page. That first line of dialogue, if there is any, can be critical to roping in a curious audience.

OPPORTUNITY

This is a very unusual and powerful branding opportunity to deliver a full line of dialogue to an audience that has initiated interest in your company by first visiting your YouTube page.

DESIGN CONSIDERATIONS

- Actually say something immediately. Don't open with just music.

- It's your chance to make a first impression. What do you think your visitors want to hear?

- The first line should entice the viewer to stick around for the second line. The second line should deepen that interest to the next line. This should continue until you've got enough material to hook them in.

CURRENT TREND

There's not much of a trend at all here. Since we didn't see any YouTube channel-specific welcoming videos, we didn't hear any first lines that specifically addressed the YouTube audience or acknowledged its location on a YouTube page.

No one appeared to put much value in that opening line as evidenced by some of the opening lines we did hear:

- "Technology touches all of us."

- "In today's digital world, the networked economy of brands, influencers, and customers, interacting across channels, has forever changed communications."

- "Here's the thing about creating what's next."

- "Twenty years ago when we first got into the server business, we were building a bridge to the future."

- "Imagine if you could build the perfect city or community."

- "Markets move quickly. Supply and demand is highly volatile. And supply chains are complex."

- "Every organization we talk to today is undergoing a major transformation to help them differentiate and be competitive in the marketplace."

- "Data protection is a heavy burden for companies to bear."

- "If you work in IT security, you know you have to keep your organization's critical assets safe."

Difficulty:

Impact:

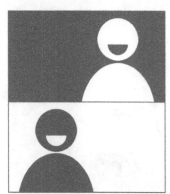

HAVE A DIFFERENT INTRO VIDEO FOR NEW VISITORS VS. SUBSCRIBERS

YouTube gives creators the opportunity to present a different video for subscribers vs. non-subscribers.

OPPORTUNITY

A new visitor is highly receptive to a welcoming video that explains the channel. Conversely, that same welcoming video or a generic branding video would annoy a returning visitor who became a subscriber. They'd want to see something new. Take advantage of the option to adapt the featured video for these two audiences. Drive new visitors to subscribe and keep your current viewers happy so they don't unsubscribe.

DESIGN CONSIDERATIONS

- For subscribers, it's often best to present the newest videos and/or latest announcements.
- For those yet to subscribe, a welcoming video that gives them reasons to subscribe is ideal (see opportunity #3).
- By not updating your page's featured video or leaving it as the same one for non-subscribers, it sends a message to your subscribers that you're simply not paying attention to the channel or to them

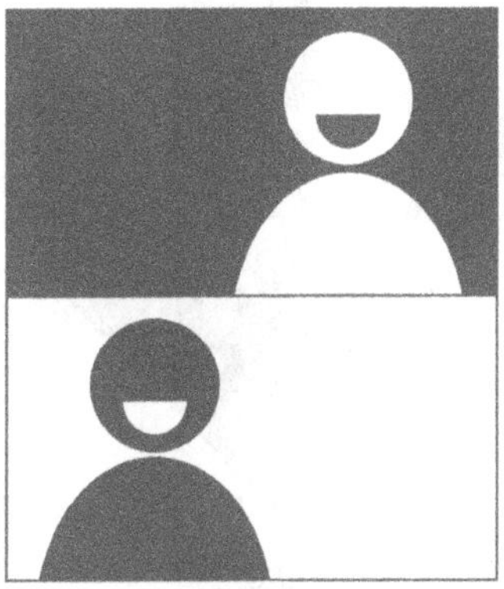

CURRENT TREND

Forty percent of all companies we looked at either didn't have or didn't bother changing the featured video for subscribers.

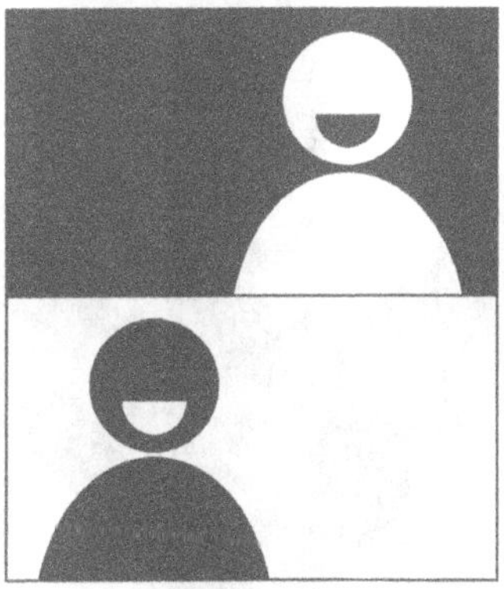

Difficulty: 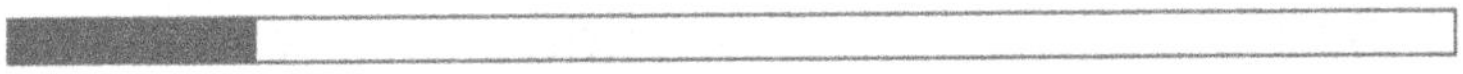

Impact: 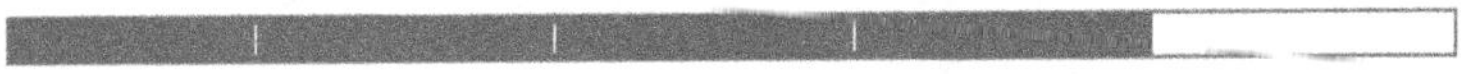

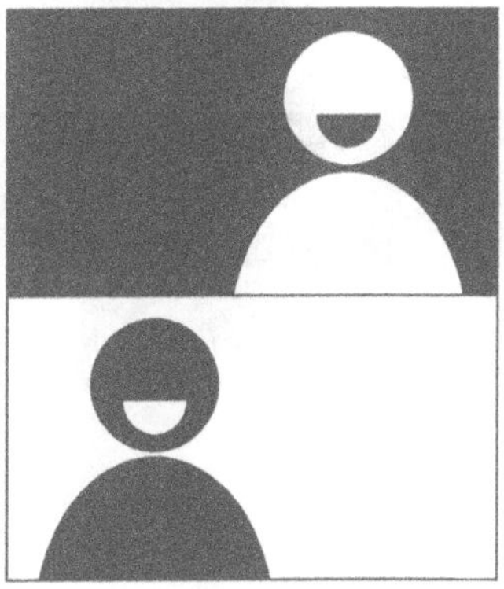

DRIVE PEOPLE TO SUBSCRIBE TO THE CHANNEL

Like any lead-gathering exercise, a unified effort across all media channels should be conducted to drive more people to subscribe to your YouTube channel. This can be done through the technical tools YouTube offers, within the content of your videos, and in external communications efforts (e.g., website, email marketing, social media).

OPPORTUNITY

Similar to having a mailing list or podcast, once you have people subscribed to your channel, you essentially have a captive and interested audience that's expecting, not bothered by, your communications.

As compared to mailing lists and podcasts, a YouTube subscriber is arguably more powerful because YouTube will feature your videos in its email marketing to its users.

DESIGN CONSIDERATIONS

- Within the production of the video, make audible and visual call-outs asking viewers to subscribe to your channel.

- Ingrain subscribe requests within the content, your company page, and email marketing. Plus, turn on all the technical features YouTube offers to make it easy for subscribers to click.

- Take advantage of all opportunities within video to get users to subscribe: subscribe button, end screens, and cards.

- Add a subscribe button in your description.

- When linking to your channel page, add *?sub_confirmation=1* to the end of your YouTube channel URL. When that code is added, anyone who clicks the link will get a prompt to subscribe to your channel (if they're not already subscribed).

CURRENT TREND

Companies go through extraordinary effort and cost to get more subscribers to their email marketing list. They will spend fortunes producing and purchasing whitepapers and sponsoring conferences. With all this attention and money spent on enticing people to "subscribe" to a marketing list, we found it surprising that the B2B organizations we looked at did not apply that same marketing tactic to their YouTube channel.

Thirty eight percent of the companies made any effort to drive more people to subscribe to their channel.

Difficulty:

Impact:

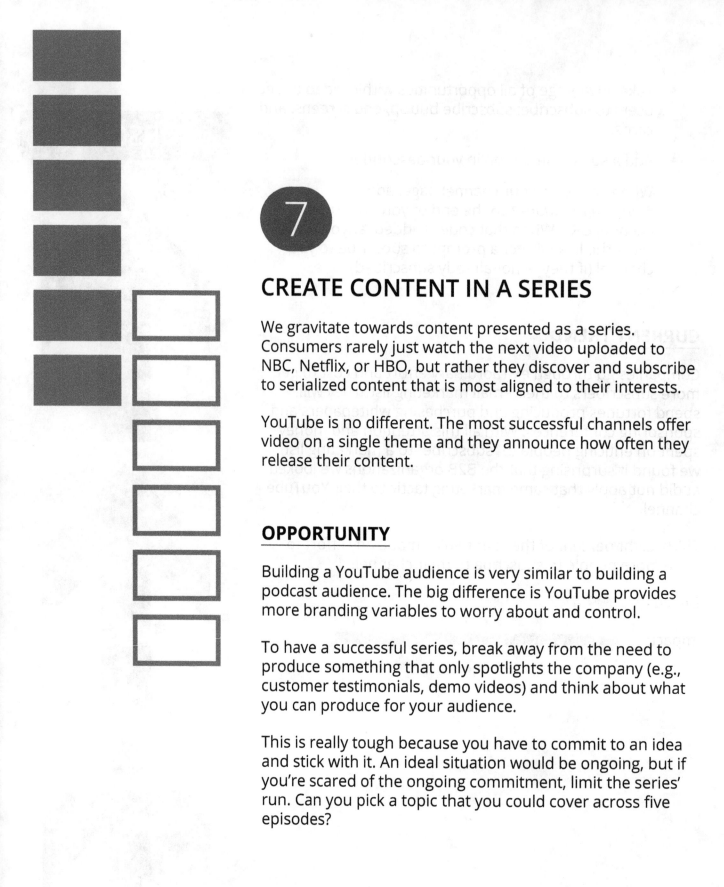

7

CREATE CONTENT IN A SERIES

We gravitate towards content presented as a series. Consumers rarely just watch the next video uploaded to NBC, Netflix, or HBO, but rather they discover and subscribe to serialized content that is most aligned to their interests.

YouTube is no different. The most successful channels offer video on a single theme and they announce how often they release their content.

OPPORTUNITY

Building a YouTube audience is very similar to building a podcast audience. The big difference is YouTube provides more branding variables to worry about and control.

To have a successful series, break away from the need to produce something that only spotlights the company (e.g., customer testimonials, demo videos) and think about what you can produce for your audience.

This is really tough because you have to commit to an idea and stick with it. An ideal situation would be ongoing, but if you're scared of the ongoing commitment, limit the series' run. Can you pick a topic that you could cover across five episodes?

DESIGN CONSIDERATIONS

- What unique expertise or access to expertise do you have that would be of interest to your audience?

- Write out episode titles so you know you have enough content to create the series.

- Make a small upfront investment to save tons of time and money in production by testing episode titles in both social media and with experimental ads. Measure responses and only create content where there's interest.

- Follow statistics and see what people are watching. If traffic is gravitating towards a certain style of content, double-down on that content and produce more.

- Develop a consistent design template across all episodes.

- Announce your production schedule in your YouTube banner and across social media (e.g., "New episodes every Thursday").

CURRENT TREND

B2B tech companies produce an endless stream of "one-off" videos that aren't connected to a larger story, explanation, or relationship-building effort with the audience.

This behavior may be the result of splintered groups all having the power to produce and publish video to the corporate YouTube channel with no management and branding oversight. While this doesn't happen at an established media property, it is the norm for all B2B tech companies presenting themselves as a media entity, specifically on YouTube.

While we never saw a case where a series commanded all the content on a corporate YouTube channel, we were pleased to see that 70 percent of the companies did have at least one significant branded series.

Difficulty: ▐▬▬▬▬▬▬▬▬▬▬▐

Impact: ▐▬▬▬▬▬▬▬▬▬▬▐

KEEP THE FRONT PAGE UPDATED WITH NEW VIDEOS

If you use an OTT (over the top) video service and you periodically log in to see what's new, you understand the excitement of seeing new content. Even if you don't watch any of the new shows, you at least know they care about the front page and you'll come back again and again to see what's new. This feeling is no different than going to a news site or blog.

Conversely, if you log in and you don't see anything new, it appears they've abandoned their site. If they don't care about their site, why should you?

OPPORTUNITIES

New content is an attractor for repeat visitors. Without it, your audience will deteriorate. YouTube provides many options to customizing your front page, such as showcasing different videos, updating your banner, and creating and reorganizing playlists.

DESIGN CONSIDERATIONS

- Show you care about subscribers by moving the most recent videos to the front page.

- Make sure to always update the featured video, especially for subscribers.

- Consider updating the banner to spotlight a recent video.

CURRENT TREND:

We saw many front pages on YouTube, especially for subscribed visitors, that showed videos that were more than two years old. But, a quick check of recently updated videos showed the company had uploaded plenty of fresh content. An omission of front page management made the site look dated.

About 1/5th of the companies didn't have any new videos to showcase. Their most recent videos were at least a year old.

Difficulty: ▇▇▇▇▇
Impact: ▇▇▇▇▇▇▇▇

PRESENT VIDEOS IN A DIGESTIBLE FORMAT

YouTube offers a reasonable amount of control in how you present your videos. Order can be had through the creation of playlists, rearranging your front page, and determining your featured video.

OPPORTUNITY

Direct visitors as to what you'd like them to see first.

If you don't organize the videos, the site looks neglected and abandoned.

DESIGN CONSIDERATIONS

- Place every video into a playlist so there's a logical structure to all assets. You don't want any "abandoned" videos.

- Create playlists to increase watch time on your channel. Consider adding only five to six videos into a playlist. Dozens of videos in a playlist can be intimidating.

- Make playlist title names descriptive and enticing. They should speak to a need or want of the viewer. For example, a playlist that just says "customer testimonials" does not entice. Retitle it to "Why sufferers of *Y* chose Company *X*."

CURRENT TREND

A good 14 percent of the organizations we looked at saw their YouTube page as just a dumping ground for whatever videos any department happened to produce.

Difficulty: ▰▰▰▰▰▱▱▱▱▱

Impact: ▰▰▰▰▰▰▱▱▱▱

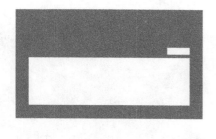

10

PUT SOCIAL CARDS AND LINKS ON THE TOP BANNER

In the upper right corner of any YouTube page is a series of social cards that allow visitors to find your company page and social profiles. When you edit your About page, the first five links you add will appear as clickable icons in the lower right corner of your banner image.

OPPORTUNITY

These icons are akin to having all your social profiles as buttons at the top of your company page.

DESIGN CONSIDERATIONS

- Only include active social profiles.

- These icons don't necessarily have to link to a social profile or company page. You can include a link to any webpage.

- If you link to a Twitter account you may not see the Twitter icon, but rather a generic globe icon.

- While only the first five links appear as icons in your banner, you can include lots more links to pages and other social profiles on your About page.

CURRENT TREND

More than half of the companies fully filled out their social profiles. While it's probably the simplest element to fix, we still found that 20 percent of the companies didn't bother to make this edit.

Difficulty:

Impact:

11

CREATE CUSTOM THUMBNAILS

Before anyone plays your video, it's just an icon waiting to be clicked. A custom thumbnail is another enticement, if not the main attractor, to get someone to click and watch your video.

A custom thumbnail is also the image that appears in the play window when your video is embedded on a webpage.

OPPORTUNITY

Not only can a custom thumbnail improve the clickability of your video, it can also provide consistent branding for your YouTube page. When all videos are presented with branded thumbnails, it looks extremely polished and professional.

Just take a look at what custom thumbnails can do to a YouTube page. We have lots of them on the Spark Media Solutions YouTube page: https://www.youtube.com/SparkMediaSolutions

Even if you didn't produce custom thumbnails when you initially produced the videos, you can still add them after the fact.

For all the opportunities presented in this document, we believe this tip provides the biggest bang for the buck/effort.

DESIGN CONSIDERATIONS

- Stay consistent with company branding guidelines.

- Make sure text is readable in small icon format.

- Provide a single standout visual along with an alert or specific call-out to the value of the video.

- Create a repeatable thumbnail template specifically for series/playlists.

CURRENT TREND

More than half of the companie didn't produce any custom thumbnails. A little more than one-fifth of the companies had well-designed custom thumbnails across almost all of their videos.

Difficulty:

Impact:

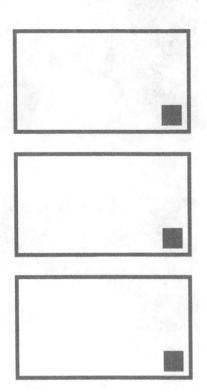

12

TURN ON AND BRAND THE SUBSCRIBE BUTTON

One YouTube feature, found in channel settings, allows for the addition of a branded watermark on top of all your YouTube videos. The watermark also doubles as a subscribe button for your YouTube channel.

OPPORTUNITY

This opportunity provides the greatest benefit in terms of ease of completion. You get branding and an automatic subscribe button across all your videos, even the ones you published years ago.

The persistent button affords an easy way for people to subscribe to your channel while watching your video, even when the video is embedded on a web page.

DESIGN CONSIDERATIONS

- The bug is a layer on top of your video. It can only appear in the lower right corner.

- For all future videos you may want to avoid adding a bug to YouTube published videos, or put the bug in any corner but the lower right corner.

- If you can, try to put the word "Subscribe" somewhere in that bug. But that may not be necessary, as it's becoming very clear to most YouTube viewers that the floating bug is a subscribe button.

CURRENT TREND

For something that is so easy to do and provides so much benefit, only 14 percent of the companies turned on this feature.

Difficulty:

Impact:

Please **SUBSCRIBE** to my video channel:
youtube.com/sparkmediasolutions

13

TAKE ADVANTAGE OF CARDS

Cards are the poke-out reminders that appear in the middle of videos and allow the viewer to click over to another relevant video while not losing their place in the current video.

OPPORTUNITY

Use cards when something mentioned in the current video references another video. Cards help extend channel watch time, which is a top YouTube metric that improves your future visibility. Cards are added within YouTube after a video is produced.

DESIGN CONSIDERATIONS

- Use sporadically. While you want to keep the viewer engaged with your current video, you still want to let the them know there's further information.

- For every video you link to through a card, add it to the YouTube description as well. The viewer may want to stay on the current video and then watch the referenced video later.

- If possible, include videos linked in the cards to the end screen as well.

CURRENT TREND

Only 16 percent of companies took advantage of using cards.

Difficulty:

Impact:

TAKE ADVANTAGE OF END SCREENS

End screens allow you to add clickable thumbnail buttons during the last 20 seconds of any video. These buttons are designed to entice viewers to stay engaged with your videos or products.

Unlike the previous incarnation of YouTube annotations, these buttons work when viewing videos on either desktop or mobile.

OPPORTUNITY

This is a clickable-within-the-video "call to action" opportunity. Push viewers to watch another video, subscribe to your channel, visit your company page, and/or purchase a product.

DESIGN CONSIDERATION

- While end screens are added after a video is produced, keep in mind the last 20 seconds of your video must be produced to make space for the end screens.

- When designing the graphics and presentation of the last 20 seconds of the video, realize that the buttons are a predetermined size and can appear only in certain areas of the screen.

- What will actually be said at the end of the video to entice people to stay engaged and click?

- While there is variability, the screen comfortably fits only four clickable buttons.

CURRENT TREND

We saw only one company that produced well-formatted interactive end screens.

Difficulty:

Impact:

DRAW VIEWERSHIP WITH ENTICING VIDEO TITLES

Along with the thumbnail image, a video's title helps persuade a viewer to click on your video.

OPPORTUNITY

For search and social visibility, a video title should be given the same care and consideration as a blog title. A descriptive title will do better in search while a dramatic clickbait title will be enticing in social media. Poor-performing videos can often be improved by rewriting the video title.

DESIGN CONSIDERATIONS

- Don't let the video title be an afterthought. Brainstorm video titles before producing the video.

- Brainstorm at least 20 video titles. This exercise forces you to dig down to the core of the audience's concerns and the answers you can deliver.

CURRENT TREND

We were really impressed with about 28 percent of the video titles we saw. Conversely, about 48 percent of the companies put little-to-no effort into writing their titles. They were minimally descriptive or were in no way tempting viewers to click and watch.

Difficulty: ▰▱▱▱▱

Impact: ▰▰▰▱▱

16

CRAFT SEARCHABLE VIDEO TITLES

As YouTube videos appear in natural search results on Google, video titles should be optimized for search.

OPPORTUNITY

Like with blog posts, your video title is critical – if not the most important variable – for search visibility.

DESIGN CONSIDERATIONS

- If I were interested in this subject, how would I find this video? What are the words that are most commonly searched?

- Take advantage of keyword research and search optimization tools to determine words that must appear in your video title.

- Utilize the same aforementioned design considerations also presented for enticing video titles.

CURRENT TREND

We believe a quarter of B2B tech companies could greatly improve the search visibility of their videos by simply rewriting the video titles.

Difficulty: ▓▓▓▓▓░░░░░░░░░░░░░░░░░░

Impact: ▓▓▓▓▓▓▓▓▓▓▓▓▓▓▓░░░░░░

17

INCLUDE TAGS TO IMPROVE SEARCH VISIBILITY

While a video title is the most useful variable to being seen in search, tags can also be used to include alternative keywords that potential viewers might use to find your video.

OPPORTUNITY

Tags are not nearly as powerful as video titles for search visibility. But they do provide some help especially if you're trying to cover your bases with similar and relevant keyword combinations. Tags can also be used for common misspellings or to identify content, products, or people in the video.

DESIGN CONSIDERATIONS

- You may want to have a standard list of tags to include in all videos for your channel. For example, producers of a YouTube channel on photography would likely tag all their videos with "photographer," "photography," and "photo." Repeating tags that appear in the video's description and title improves search visibility.

- Include your brand name in the list of tags.

- Type keywords into YouTube search and pick out the auto-suggested options as possible tags.

- Using a tool like TubeBuddy or vidIQ, you can conduct further research and appropriate tags from similar videos.

CURRENT TREND

More than one-third of the companies we looked at did a great or excellent job writing out the tags for each video. The rest of the companies did not add tags at all or made a barely passable effort.

Difficulty:

Impact:

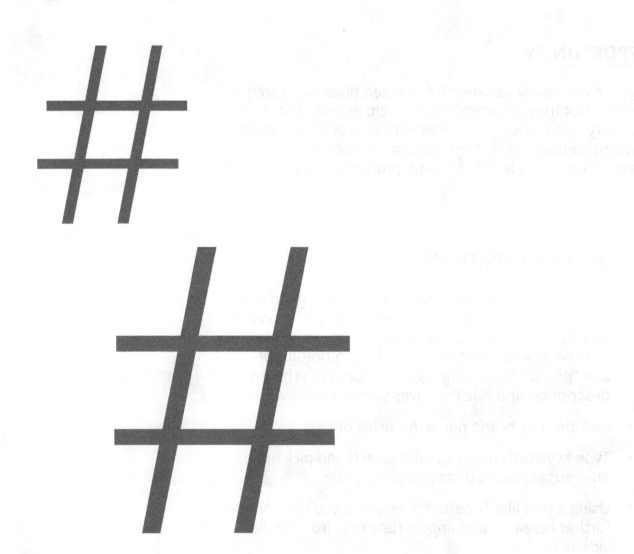

WRITE VALUABLE VIDEO DESCRIPTIONS

Second to the video title, a video's description is the most search-friendly copy you can add to a video.

OPPORTUNITY

With a relevant written description, Google has more content to index for search.

DESIGN CONSIDERATIONS

- Pay particular attention to the first few lines of the video descriptions as that is what is seen directly below the video before the user has to click "more" to see the rest of the description.

- Pay even greater attention to the first few words and first line, as that's the description seen in Google search results.

- If a blog post is written for the video, you could possibly copy and paste that content into the YouTube description.

CURRENT TREND

A whopping 86 percent of the companies we looked at should spend time rewriting their descriptions.

Difficulty: �▰▱▱▱▱

Impact: ▰▰▱▱▱

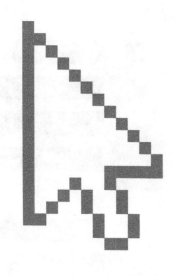

19

PROVIDE LINKS IN THE VIDEO DESCRIPTION

Links within the video description can send users to specific "calls to action" such as company pages, social profiles, company products, or additional videos.

OPPORTUNITY

Drive viewers to where you want them to go next.

DESIGN CONSIDERATIONS

- Place the links in order of preference.
- Create a template of links to company page, social links, and subscribe to channel that will appear at the bottom of every video's description.

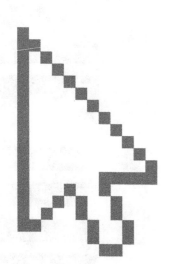

CURRENT TREND

Forty four percent of companies had little-to-no links in the descriptions. By not directing viewers "where to go next," B2B tech companies are missing an opportunity to move viewers to another branding engagement location after watching the video.

Difficulty:

Impact:

20

SOLICIT AND RESPOND TO COMMENTS AND QUESTIONS

YouTube, like all social media, should not be treated as a broadcast medium. Its commenting system affords a built-in feedback loop. Comments create engaged viewers, which turns them into passionate viewers. By watching your videos and commenting, your audience shows they care about you. More importantly, those commenters are raising their hand saying, "I'm passionate about this topic." Responding to those comments demonstrates to your audience that you care about their opinions.

OPPORTUNITY

YouTube comments are an engagement trigger, which shows a high correlation to search visibility. It's debatable as to whether YouTube includes comments in its rankings, but videos with lots of comments usually have many views and long view times, which is the top factor that increases your video's search visibility.

Find moments within the video itself to ask for feedback. More comments indicates greater engagement, thus helping to guide future production.

Respond to all comments to let your audience know that you're listening and you're responsive.

DESIGN CONSIDERATIONS

- Make explicit and specific requests for engagement in both the video and in the YouTube description. You could simply remind them to leave their opinions in the comments section, but you'll get more of a response with more unique and personal requests.

- Requests that invite lots of responses are controversial debates, opinions, sharing personal experiences, and requests for content they'd like to see in future videos.

- Make the request for comment simple. Don't ask for too much.

- Not only can you respond to comments via text, you can respond to comments in future videos. Let the audience know their responses can and will be part of future content.

- To get a velocity of comments in a short period of time, hold a contest with a time limit (e.g., "I'm giving away _____. The five best responses to this question will win. You have 72 hours to respond from the moment this video is published.")

- Make requests for comments across all social media. For example, post your video on Twitter and add "Let me know what you think in the comments on YouTube."

- Given the fleeting nature of Snapchat, it's a great platform to make requests for responses to your YouTube videos.

CURRENT TREND

Only six percent of companies were responsive to video comments. Seventy eight percent of companies were completely non-responsive to comments, got no comments on their videos, or actually turned comments off. Universally, we didn't see any company truly asking their audience to engage.

If your company realizes the importance of engaging with your audience in social media, why wouldn't you also do it on YouTube? We were surprised to see that those companies who turned off their comments on YouTube were active on other social media platforms.

Difficulty:

Impact:

21

CREATE AND MANAGE PLAYLISTS TO INCREASE WATCHTIME

Content needs to be organized, and the best way to do this on YouTube is through playlists.

OPPORTUNITY

Make sense of your video collection not just for your audience, but for yourselves as well. Playlists give structure and increases viewing time to your YouTube channel, which drives up search visibility and recommendations.

DESIGN CONSIDERATIONS

- Group your playlists by audience interest. For example, it's extremely common to create playlists of all content from a single event. Problem is that event may have multiple tracks covering lots of different content. Instead of putting all 25 videos from the same event in one playlist, split up the videos to mimic the different tracks of content you had at your event.

- YouTube allows you to manually order videos logically within the playlist. This is especially necessary if you produce "how to" videos.

- Keep the number of videos within a playlist short. Too many videos (e.g., 20+) may overwhelm the viewer from wanting to click. Try to create playlists of six or fewer videos.

CURRENT TREND

The majority of companies did a pretty good job with their playlists, with more than a third producing spectacular playlists. Some companies were truly obsessive about the process, making sure that every video produced had its place within a playlist. On the other side of the equation, companies barely understood how to use playlists or completely forgot about their existence and abandoned them.

In a few cases, companies that produced thousands of videos would put 80 to 100 videos in a single playlist, which we found extremely intimidating.

Difficulty:

Impact:

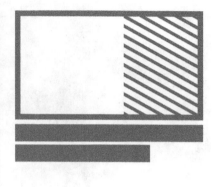

BE CREATIVE WHEN TITLING PLAYLISTS

Companies need to put the same care into writing playlist titles as they do for the titles of blog posts or videos.

OPPORTUNITY

As a visitor will click on a video that has an enticing title, the same is true for a tempting playlist title.

DESIGN CONSIDERATIONS

- Get yourself out of the bubble of looking at your playlists as titles for folders on your hard drive (e.g., Case Studies, Product X, Event Y, Testimonials). Instead of titling a playlist "Customer Success Stories," try "Customers Who Switched to *Product X*."

- A playlist title can be mysterious or lead a viewer down a path to learn more about a subject.

CURRENT TREND

Unfortunately, only 8 percent of the companies did an excellent job titling their playlists. We think the reason for the lack of care with creative titling has to do with companies looking at playlists as solely an organization mechanism and not a means to attract and extend viewership.

Difficulty:

Impact:

23

GET CREATIVE WITH PLAYLIST DESCRIPTIONS TOO

Just like you can write a description for a video, you can and should write descriptions for playlists.

OPPORTUNITY

A description is just another small way to improve the search visibility of your videos.

DESIGN CONSIDERATIONS

- Unlike a video description, a playlist description should be shorter. We suggest about two lines.
- Use the description to call out the specific content of the videos in the playlist.

CURRENT TREND

We believe that most companies simply don't know they can add a playlist description, as 70 percent of the channels had little-to-no playlist descriptions.

Difficulty:

Impact:

CREATE PLAYLISTS OF NON-COMPANY VIDEOS

Playlists need not include only videos you've produced.

OPPORTUNITY

If you have an active community, chances are they're producing videos about you and your products. Highlight them in a playlist to show that you're paying attention to your community, especially when they pay attention to you.

DESIGN CONSIDERATIONS

- Create playlists whenever your company is mentioned in the news or your employees are interviewed by other YouTubers.

- Create playlists of YouTubers reviewing your products. Be open to adding playlists of critical reviews.

- Make sure to let YouTubers know that you've added their videos to a playlist. Comment on the videos you've added.

- Create playlists of partners' videos, especially the ones that show how they interface with your company/ product.

CURRENT TREND

We saw only a couple meager attempts at this. We simply don't believe this is on anyone's radar. Unlike other social platforms, such as LinkedIn, Twitter, and Facebook, where companies regularly share other people's content, companies are still having a hard time viewing YouTube as a social network even though it's the second largest one after Facebook. Most companies view YouTube purely as a publishing platform for distribution.

Difficulty:

Impact:

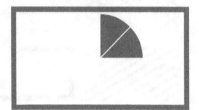
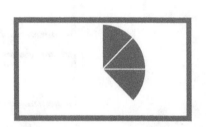

25

PUT LINKS WITHIN DESCRIPTION TO KEY MOMENTS IN THE VIDEO

For very long videos on YouTube that have lots of descriptive content, you can provide links to specific moments in the video within the description of the video.

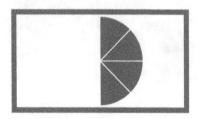

OPPORTUNITY

While this does take time to do, it's of enormous benefit to viewers who would be intimidated and/or simply don't have the time to watch a one-hour video. Let the viewer quickly get to the content they want by providing a link to that moment in the video.

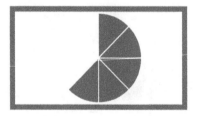

By adding linked time stamps, it avoids the laborious task of slicing up a long video into multiple shorter videos and publishing each one individually. Links to moments within a video behaves like a playlist, but better, by making it extremely easy for the viewer to jump to relevant moments within a video. They will have a longer and more enjoyable viewing experience, as compared to a long video that they'll abandon quickly out of frustration of not knowing what's in the video and where.

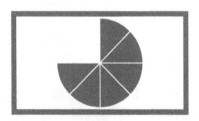

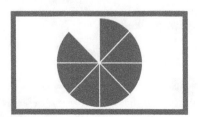

DESIGN CONSIDERATIONS

- When you're producing the video, simply write down the time stamps of the different topic changes. When you publish the video on YouTube, it will be very easy to add these links.

- Seriously consider doing this for all presentation videos at live events.

CURRENT TREND

We saw only one example of a company providing links within a video description. We believe this is a case of companies not knowing this can be done, or simply not putting in the time during and after post-production to include these time stamps and links.

Difficulty: ▰▰▰▱▱▱▱▱▱▱

Impact: ▰▰▰▰▱▱▱▱▱▱

26

MANAGE THE FRONT PAGE

We have covered all the recommended opportunities to improve your YouTube presence.

- Playlists
- Banner image
- Featured video (subscribers vs. non-subscribers)
- First words heard in featured video
- New videos
- Thumbnails
- Video titles
- Organization of videos
- Social cards on top banner

These are the elements that make up the front page of your YouTube site.

OPPORTUNITY

Coordinating all these elements is your chance to make a great first impression. This is not a "set it and forget it" option. It has to be managed over time. Frequency of management depends on how much video content you're producing.

DESIGN CONSIDERATIONS

- What is the experience you want people to feel when they hit your YouTube page?

- Think digestible, not overwhelming.

- After you fix all the above elements, do a little focus group testing with some industry colleagues. What's their first impression? What do they think this site delivers? What would they click on first?

- Remember to periodically update your YouTube front page. You don't want it to look neglected.

CURRENT TREND

About 30 percent of the companies we looked at neglected or did absolutely nothing to manage their YouTube front page. Conversely, about 20 percent of the companies did an excellent job managing their YouTube page.

We saw two common problems with YouTube page design.

First were the companies that never updated the front page

When the most recent video is a year old or older, it appears as if the YouTube site has been abandoned. This is often not the case. We'll see companies that are producing plenty of current videos, they're just forgetting to update them on their YouTube front page.

The second issue was with the largest of the Fortune 500 companies that were generating thousands of videos. Their YouTube organization tactic was to overwhelm the visitor with far too much information. Those companies had dozens of menu items with nested playlists showing dozens if not hundreds of videos. This isn't inviting. It's intimidating. No company would put up with that kind of user experience on their company website, but had no problem doing it on their YouTube page.

Difficulty: ▰▰▰▱▱▱▱

Impact: ▰▰▰▰▰▰▱

27

DRIVE LONGER CHANNEL WATCH TIME

Many of the aforementioned suggestions, such as serialized content, playlists, increased subscriptions, cards, end screens, and soliciting audience engagement, are all designed to increase channel watch time.

"The watch journey on YouTube is designed as a pathway to viewer loyalty and long-term recurrence," said Jim Louderback, CEO, VidCon (now part of Viacom).

OPPORTUNITY

Contrary to common belief, view counts are not the best metric to determine search and discovery relevance. Views and video likes can easily be gamed through bots and advertising. Above all else, YouTube prioritizes watch time for its search and discovery algorithms.

Increasing watch time is not just about getting people to watch one video longer, but also getting people to watch more videos for a longer period time across your entire channel.

DESIGN CONSIDERATIONS

- Driving longer watch time is just like a branding effort. You're aiming for a unified message across all your video efforts to entice people to watch longer.

- Craft videos where it's necessary to watch additional videos to get the full story. This can be best done when developing a training series.

- Use cards and end screens to extend view time with call-outs to relevant videos.

- Talk directly to the viewer. Push them to subscribe and ask for feedback. As compared to non-subscribers, your subscribers spend more time watching your content.

- When you put down a two-dollar bet on a horse race, you become more invested in the outcome of the race. You start to care. You can affect that same behavior in video if you can entice your audience to invest a little of themselves by sharing an opinion. Use those responses in follow-up videos and make sure those viewers see it, as it will entice them to continue viewing and participating.

CURRENT TREND

While organizations are sporadically taking advantage of all the elements to drive longer channel watch time, we didn't see even one organization looking at extending watch time as a branding effort.

Difficulty:

Impact:

TAKE ADVANTAGE OF VIDEO SUGGESTIONS

After a video finishes, YouTube will offer up some suggested videos to watch next. These suggested videos also appear on the right-hand column while the video is playing. Up until April 2017, YouTube guaranteed placements of suggested videos from the same channel as the video you're watching. Lack of this now comes to great consternation of YouTubers as suggested videos are the greatest source of additional video views.

TubeBuddy has a statistic that measures how many of the suggested videos are from the same channel as the video you're watching. This statistic varies depending on who is watching the video and their viewing history.

OPPORTUNITY

As mentioned, suggested videos are the greatest source of video traffic. The more you can get your videos suggested, the more views you'll have of your videos across your channel, which hopefully will also increase your channel watch time thereby improving search and discovery.

DESIGN CONSIDERATIONS

- Suggested videos usually have similar content. The more related content you have, the better.

- Aim to produce short series of six to eight videos. Indicate the relations with similar content in titles, descriptions, and tags. Include cards and end screens to manually drive viewers to the other videos in the series.

CURRENT TREND

While this statistic varies by viewer, we generally found middling success with creator suggested videos. About 25 percent of channels had really impressive numbers of their channel videos being suggested.

Difficulty:

Impact:

29

WRITE AN INVITING "ABOUT" PAGE

Companies have an "About" page on their website. You can also have an "About" page on your YouTube site.

OPPORTUNITY

Go beyond the simple boilerplate description on your business site and take a few minutes to write a paragraph explaining the value of your company's video channel. You can also use this space to add links to the company website and social channels.

DESIGN CONSIDERATIONS

- The "About" page is an opportunity to explain the mission of your YouTube channel.

- There are no limits on the number of links you can add. Order though does matter, though, as the first five will appear as icons in the lower right corner of your channel's banner image.

CURRENT TREND

It didn't surprise us that 44 percent of companies just pasted in their website's boilerplate copy into the YouTube channel's "About" page. Eight percent of companies left the page blank. Conversely, six percent of the companies really understood the uniqueness of the page and wrote a custom piece that explained the value proposition of their channel.

Difficulty: ▮▮▯▯▯▯▯▯▯▯▯▯▯▯▯▯▯▯▯▯

Impact: ▮▮▯▯▯▯▯▯▯▯▯▯▯▯▯▯▯▯▯▯

30

BOLSTER VIDEO REACH WITH CAPTIONS

While YouTube will make an attempt to automatically caption your videos, they are never a match for professionally and accurately produced captions.

OPPORTUNITY

Captions are not just for the hearing impaired. They're necessary, especially on Facebook, as 85 percent of video views are played without sound.[15] And Facebook claims that the presence of captions increases watch time by 12 percent. Since overall watch time is the most important variable to determine the success of a YouTube channel and that it only costs a dollar a minute to produce mostly accurate captions, it's an easy and smart choice to caption all of your videos.

DESIGN CONSIDERATIONS

- Take advantage of a service like Rev.com which will create caption files and also automatically upload them to your video on your YouTube channel.

- Even though you're paying for caption files, they're rarely 100 percent accurate. Make sure you watch the videos and edit the caption files as needed.

- Save the .srt file with an additional extension for your language and country so you can upload the same caption file to Facebook. For example, for English-speaking viewers in the United States you would add the extension *.en_US.srt*.

CURRENT TREND

This is a simple and cheap decision that provides a big impact, but 70 percent of the channels we surveyed had little-to-no captions. Six percent of the channels had almost all of their videos captioned.

Difficulty: ▓▓▓░░░░░░░░░░░░░░░░

Impact: ▓▓▓▓▓▓▓▓▓▓▓▓░░░░░

TURN ON CAPTIONS BY DEFAULT

If you upload captions to YouTube, you can turn them on by default.

OPPORTUNITY

Once you have created and uploaded captions, simply add the tag *yt:cc=on* to automatically turn on captions for that particular video. As previously mentioned, captions increase viewing time. This is especially true on sites such as LinkedIn and Facebook that play videos automatically without sound in their respective news feeds.

DESIGN CONSIDERATIONS

- Best to turn on captions by default for talking head videos.

- Uploading captions to a Facebook video turns them on by default. They turn off when a viewer initiates play, which turns on the audio.

- Captions are often not necessary for videos that:

  · Already have a lot of animated text.

  · Are more visual and have very little talking.

  · Have lots of information in the lower third of the screen. The presence of captions would be an intrusion and would cover up that information.

CURRENT TREND

Close to 80 percent of the channels we looked at did not turn on captions ever. The other 20 percent had only a handful of videos that either turned on closed captions by default, or had open captions, which are burned directly onto the video.

Difficulty:

Impact:

32

ACCURATELY LABEL ADVERTISEMENTS

It's quite OK to post commercials to your YouTube channel. Conversely, it's not OK to try to pass off an advertisement as content.

OPPORTUNITY

Don't try to fool your audience when you're trying to build trust. Simply label advertisements as advertisements. Most people are going to YouTube for informational or entertaining content. You may believe your commercials are entertaining, but in general, viewers don't want to be watching a video to all of a sudden find out they're watching a commercial. It's not a good user experience.

DESIGN CONSIDERATIONS

- Video title should begin with *AD:*

- Unlike TV programming, don't create playlists that mix editorial content with advertisements.

- Create playlists for your advertisements and label them as such.

CURRENT TREND

Only 76 percent of the companies we looked at had advertisements on their YouTube page. Of that group, 48 percent did not label their advertisements, and we saw only six percent accurately labeled.

Difficulty: ▰▱▱▱▱

Impact: ▰▰▱▱▱

PUBLISH CURRENT CONTENT

A site with current content has energy and lures subscribers. Viewing a YouTube channel with no new videos is just like seeing an outdated blog.

YouTube avidly promotes channels that constantly turn out fresh content.

OPPORTUNITY

You can drive more subscribers with consistent and frequent publishing of content. In addition, with each piece of content you upload, YouTube will promote that content to your subscribers on YouTube's front page and also in their email marketing.

DESIGN CONSIDERATIONS

- Producing content consistently is not easy. Don't take on more than you can handle.

- Two ways to produce content consistently is to have something programmatic shot with static equipment (camera, lighting, mikes) or shoot lots of content in batches (easy to do at live events).

CURRENT TREND

Half of the companies we looked at were doing an excellent job creating enough current content to populate their YouTube channel. Those companies falling short were not necessarily poorly funded.

Difficulty: ████████████████████████

Impact: ████████████████████████

34

TAKE ADVANTAGE OF IMMEDIACY OF YOUTUBE CONTENT PROMOTION

YouTube promotes videos that have been published within the last seven days.

OPPORTUNITY

When YouTube highlights your video for its visitors and your subscribers, go out of your way to do as much paid or organic (e.g., email marketing, social) promotion as you can during that first week. After the first week, the video's popularity may inevitably drop, but increased traffic in a video's first week of release will improve its future discoverability.

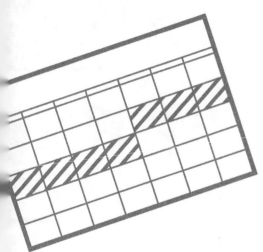

CONSIDERATIONS

- Have a promotion plan in place before you publish your video.

- Keep this in mind for all your videos. Poor video velocity on one upload can actually impact the discoverability of your next uploads.

- Be wary of any consultant who promises you top ranking in search within 24 hours. Your video will probably rank in search that first 24 hours just because it's new. But because of YouTube's freshness algorithm, that popularity simply won't last.

CURRENT TREND

About half of the companies we looked at took advantage of YouTube's golden period to promote their videos. Those organizations that chose not to promote during this window often received less than 100 views for their videos in the first 72 hours even though they had thousands of subscribers.

Difficulty:

Impact:

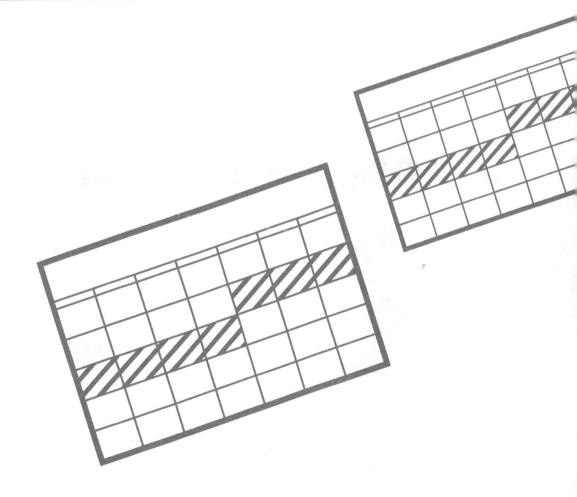

35

SHARE VIDEOS WITHIN A YOUTUBE PLAYLIST

When you post a video share the link to that video within its respective playlist instead of just a direct link to that specific video. When a viewer finishes the video within a playlist, the next video in your playlist will play, instead of some random video recommended by YouTube.

OPPORTUNITY

Sharing a video's playlist link is a simple solution to help extend your channel view time. All you have to do is simply link to or embed the playlist version of your video.

DESIGN CONSIDERATIONS

Keep your playlists short, just 4-6 videos. Any more could potentially be overwhelming.

CURRENT TREND

While it was difficult to measure this, we didn't see any examples of the studied companies linking to or embedding the playlist versions of their videos.

Difficulty:

Impact:

Other Video Issues

36

PUBLISH LONG-FORM VIDEOS

Data shows that people will watch long-form content. In fact, it's preferred. Starting in 2017, long-form video content won the most watch time across TVs, PCs, and mobile devices.[16]

OPPORTUNITY

Don't be afraid to create long-form content. The average length of a first page YouTube video is 14 minutes, 50 seconds.[17] We've fooled ourselves into believing that people have short attention spans and won't watch a video more than three minutes. That's true if the video is boring or pure marketing fluff. If compelling, entertaining, and/or delivers on the information desired, people will watch.

You don't need a viewer to consume the entire video for it to be successful. As we've mentioned, YouTube's greatest success metric is watch time. Sixty-five percent of video viewers watch more than 3/4th of a video.[18]

DESIGN CONSIDERATIONS

- There are plenty of video formats that lend themselves to long-form video:

  · Presentations

  · Webinars

  · Panel discussions

  · Interviews

  · Explanations of complicated processes

- If posting on YouTube, provide a better viewing experience by adding links to specific moments in the video to allow the viewer to jump around to just the part of the video that most interests them. For more, see opportunity number 25, "Put links within description to key moments in the video."

CURRENT TREND

A little more than 75 percent of the channels we looked at took advantage of producing videos that were more than ten minutes long. The other quarter almost never broke the three-minute barrier.

These long-form videos were almost always produced cheaply as either presentations, interviews, or panel discussions.

Difficulty:

Impact:

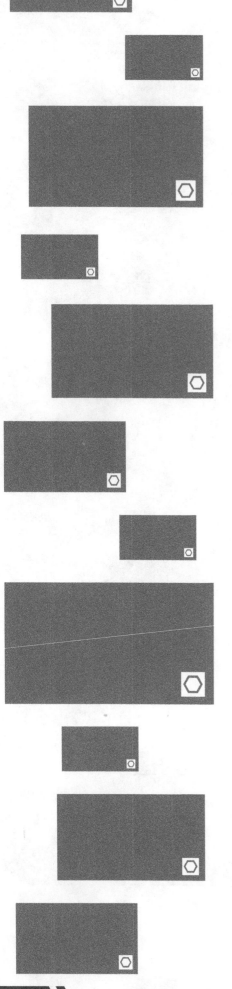

37

PRODUCE VIDEOS CONSISTENT WITH CORPORATE BRANDING

Match the video quality, tone, and graphics with the rest of the company's corporate branding.

OPPORTUNITY

This falls under the "must do" category. You must transfer the company's financial and creative investment in branding over to video production. Not doing this can severely damage your brand.

DESIGN CONSIDERATIONS

- Design a video template (opening and closing slides, lower thirds, text graphics, and other graphic treatments) that is consistent with the corporate style guide.

- Publish this style guide on the company intranet. Make sure all departments use that same video template. Brands do change over time, so make sure to update the video template to reflect that.

- Create a video style guide that not only explains how to use the template, but also states the tone you expect to strike with your videos and the relationship you want to have with your audience.

CURRENT TREND

Here's where we saw some of the most dramatic failures. Less than half of the companies did a great to excellent job tying corporate branding to their videos; the rest, which was a narrow majority, desperately needed help improving their video branding. We even saw this with Fortune 500 tech companies.

Given that brands evolve over time, controlling video branding is not as easy as updating a blog or website. Regardless, the issue that we saw often, especially with large companies, is they lacked consistency in their graphics packages and content style. What we believe is happening is different departments are hiring different video production crews that are generating completely different graphics templates with a variety of different branding elements.

Difficulty: �

Impact: ▮▮▮▮

38

FUND VIDEOS APPROPRIATELY

The cost of a video can vary from nothing to tens of thousands, if not hundreds of thousands, of dollars. That cost is dependent on a variety of variables such as company brand, video objective, talent, and the situation in which the video is shot.

OPPORTUNITY

Since there are so many variables that determine how much you should spend on a video, feel free to experiment with how you produce videos, taking into consideration all the aforementioned variables. Remember that not all videos are equal. Some require more funding than others.

DESIGN CONSIDERATIONS

- If you're capturing the energy around a live event, it's actually OK to produce a low-cost mobile phone streaming video.

- As long as the content in the video has value, you can skimp on post-production flash.

- Never skimp on audio and lighting. Without it, your video becomes nearly unwatchable and thereby brand damaging.

CURRENT TREND

A little more than a quarter of the companies did not understand the concept of appropriately funded videos. Even with Fortune 500 companies, we saw highly produced animated videos right next to videos that had poor lighting and sound. We also saw a few cases of unnecessarily overproduced videos.

Difficulty:

Impact:

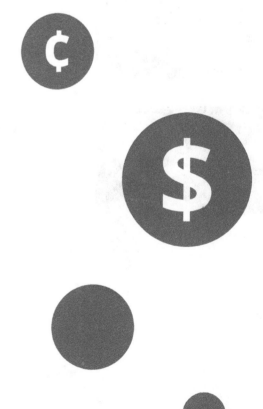

EMBRACE VIDEO VARIETY

Does your company have one format that's consistently working for them? Or are you experimenting with different styles, giving the audience alternatives, trying to do something unique to set you apart from competition?

OPPORTUNITY

Just because a certain video is easy to produce (webinars and presentations) and it's what every other tech company produces (case studies, customer interviews, animated demos), it doesn't mean that you're required by B2B video content marketing law to create the same thing. Experiment with a variety of different styles.

DESIGN CONSIDERATIONS

- Before you produce the video, ask yourself, "Are you producing this video because it's expected?" or "Are you producing this video because there's a specific audience that wants to see it?"

- Have a creative brainstorming session. Maybe there's another more original way to tell the same story.

- Work from the end result. At the end of this video, I want people to do _____. What would you have to produce to get them to do that?

CURRENT TREND

Video variety vs. lack of video variety was evenly distributed across all companies. We saw the epitome of bland (webcasts and commercials) to funny videos and creative takes on current trends.

Difficulty:

Impact:

40

INJECT HUMANITY AND/OR HUMOR

Companies that want to show they're different and have a more human culture will go out of their way to break from producing the same generic corporate video.

OPPORTUNITY

Given social interactions, online video affords you the ability to create people-to-people connections. When people purchase a product, they're not hoping for a dry corporate video.

If you believe the trope of "people sell to people," then you must inject humanity into your videos. This is most critical when you're producing employer-brand videos that convey corporate culture.

DESIGN CONSIDERATIONS

- Try to avoid using stock footage, or if you're going to use it, make sure you stylize it to your specific needs.

- Look for talent in-house. Who are the most engaging employees who would be great on camera?

- If you're investing in major marketing campaigns, look for talent outside who can deliver the key messages you want with humor. We saw companies who made this investment and it appears to have paid off.

CURRENT TREND

About 14 percent of the companies we looked at did an amazing job with humor in their videos. It wasn't all their videos, but they selectively decided to hire great, sometimes A-list, talent to appear in their corporate videos.

Forty percent of the companies we looked at did little to nothing to inject humor and/or humanity into their videos. We believe they were running through a rubber stamp model of here are the videos "we have to create."

Difficulty:

Impact:

GO BEYOND THE SIZZLE REEL

Just like everyone feels they must have an 8 ½" x 11" one-page paper resume, every company that produces an event feels they need to have a sizzle reel. Neither are necessary. Sizzle reels are videos composed of imagery and positive memes often completely devoid of information. And while the video producer may think they're being original and eye-catching, the reality is content from one sizzle reel could be exchanged with another and it wouldn't change either video.

OPPORTUNITY

If you're producing an event, stop making self-indulgent sizzle reels that are all about you, the event producer, and not the attendees. If there's so much amazing content coming out of your event, then why not create a video about that?

DESIGN CONSIDERATIONS

- Show. Don't tell people that it's an amazing event.

- If everyone's sizzle reel shows people dancing, waving glow sticks, and telling you that there are really great conversations at this event, then you need to show the uniqueness and value of your event.

- If you program so much content into your event, why not provide highlights in a summary video?

- Two alternatives that capture the buzz of an event that we produce at Spark Media Solutions are funny "man on the street" style videos and "end of show" report videos. Both formats showcase the attendees and speakers, and their wisdom. For more, read my article, 21 Tips for Producing Funny "Man on the Street" Videos.

CURRENT TREND

A little more than half of all the companies we looked at didn't produce events, therefore had no need to produce a sizzle reel. For all the other companies that did produce events, about a third broke away from the traditional sizzle reel. The other two-thirds created the same dazzling yet redundant display. None of those videos showed any of the content from the event.

Difficulty:

Impact:

CAPTURE VIDEO ENGAGEMENT

If you don't monetize your videos through views, you shouldn't care about viewcounts at all. Let's say you got thousands of views on a video. What does that mean? What can you do with it?

To a B2B company, knowing who is watching a video, when they watched it, and for how long is far more valuable information.

OPPORTUNITY

Start using an interactive video platform such as Brightcove, Vidyard, or Wistia that allows you to measure who consumes what, and when, and for how long. More importantly, these programs allow you to create interactive videos with calls-to-action that can be sent directly to your email marketing or marketing automation program. For a B2B audience, knowing the few people who actually watched all your videos and cared about them is far more powerful to your sales staff than showing that a specific video got thousands of views.

DESIGN CONSIDERATIONS

- Produce videos where there are enticements to watch more. For example, 45 seconds into a video you could have the host say, "Stay tuned, we're going to show you exactly how we do this." At that point you could stop the video with a message on the screen that says, "If you'd like to see how he actually does this, enter your email address." This method of gatekeeping can allow for continuous tracking of viewership whenever they return to watch your videos.

- Make sure to have a measurement and follow-up process with those individuals who have spent the most time watching and engaging with your videos.

CURRENT TREND

About 70 percent of the companies we looked at appeared to have no targeted action plan for how they were going to follow-up with viewers.

Difficulty: ▰▰▰▰▰▰▰▱

Impact: ▰▰▰▰▰▰▰▰

43

GET TO THE CONTENT RIGHT AWAY

Twenty percent of your audience will disappear within the first 10 seconds of playback. A third will be gone before thirty seconds.[19] If you have long introductions in your videos or you're wasting time not getting to the point, you're aggravating that statistic.

OPPORTUNITY

If you're fortunate enough to get people to click on your video, don't alienate them with sloppy video production. One of the dangers of video, unlike reading a blog posts, is that it just takes a few seconds for people to pass judgment on the quality and value of your video. Viewers won't wait for your video to get better.

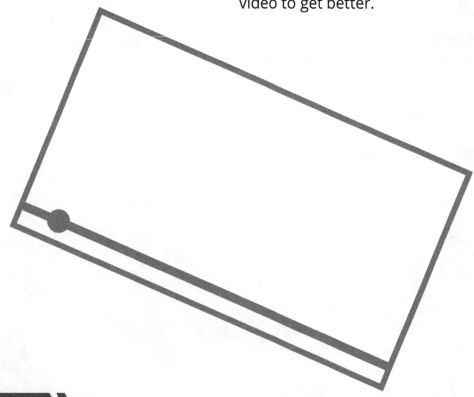

DESIGN CONSIDERATIONS

- Make sure you have good audio and lighting. If either is poor, your viewer will instantly become frustrated and bail.

- Don't waste time with long introductions.

- Use the tease-deliver-tease model of production. Tell them what you're going to deliver, and then deliver it. But, as you deliver that piece of information, tease them with something else that keeps them hanging on. One easy format for doing this is a list. If you create a top 10 list and only make it available on video, your audience will be anxiously watching to see what the next item on the list will be.

CURRENT TREND

We saw an even distribution between companies that do a great job getting to the point and those that waste far too much time. Half though were smack in the middle. They weren't horrible, but they had plenty of room for improvement.

Difficulty: ▮▮▮▮▮▮▯▯▯▯

Impact: ▮▮▮▮▮▮▮▮▯▯

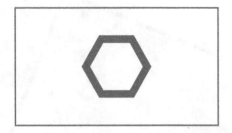

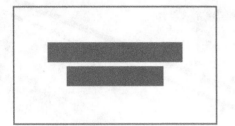

44

MAKE SHORT OPENING ANIMATIONS

It's common and appropriate for a company to produce a short opening animation as a video identifier. You see these on networks to identify which network you're watching. A quick animation or stinger is usually less than four seconds.

OPPORTUNITY

Given the concern of losing people in the first ten seconds, it's imperative to not waste this time with an unnecessarily long opening animation. While you want some type of branded identifier, design it so it does its job in just a few seconds.

DESIGN CONSIDERATIONS

- If you put a bug in the corner, you don't necessarily need an opening animation. Your video identifier is with the bug. But, opening animations are great for building brand awareness.

- Keep the opening animation as short as possible. Three seconds is ideal.

- Try to avoid opening the video with the opening animation. Throw in some type of teaser as to what the video is, and then show the animation.

- As you create a video style guide, provide the asset to the opening animation and explain proper uses and when it's OK not to use it.

CURRENT TREND

More than half of the companies we looked at had very short opening animations. About 14 percent had animations that were unnecessarily long.

Difficulty:

Impact:

PROVIDE EDUCATIONAL/TRAINING VIDEOS

You've got customers and they want to know how to use your products. One easy way to answer that call for help is to create training and support videos.

OPPORTUNITY

This is one of those cases where you can truly calculate a return on investment for video. If you have a list of frequently asked questions (FAQs) for which you're still getting support requests, augment those FAQ answers with a video-based FAQ. If you release a video that better explains and shows how to solve a problem it will save both time and money at your call center and support desk. What's the cost to produce those videos? How many calls do you get that could be answered by that video? Calculate that time and the cost for that time. How many months of customer support time does it take to pay for the production of those videos?

DESIGN CONSIDERATIONS

- To determine which videos to make first, ask your customer service and tech support departments what are the top ten questions and requests they get. Which requests take the most time to answer?

- If you're showing off physical equipment, make sure to do extreme close-ups and have excellent lighting.

- Costly production is often not necessary. The person just wants an answer. For software explanations, a simple screencast video can show off the most common issues.

CURRENT TREND

Almost two-thirds of the companies did a great-to-excellent job producing training videos. For those companies, many created completely separate YouTube channels just to host the training videos.

Difficulty: ██████████████████████

Impact: ████████████████████████

46

AVOID PRODUCING CONTENT-FREE VIDEOS

A content-free video is a video that provides zero information. Commercials on a YouTube channel often fall into this category. Another common example of a valueless video is one that teases information that's never delivered. The most egregious case of this is a live event video where on-camera hosts tell you that a specific person spoke at the event, but they don't provide any highlights as to what was said.

OPPORTUNITY

Before you produce or publish a video, ask yourself, "What's the value of this video?" A corporate video doesn't necessarily have to inform. It can be entertaining, funny, or visually stunning. But if it's none of those, don't produce it and don't post it.

CONSIDERATIONS

- Avoid alienating your audience by producing self-indulgent videos that make the people on camera feel good about being on camera.

- Content-free videos often occur when a company treats their YouTube channel as a dumping ground for whatever video they happen to produce.

CURRENT TREND

The problem with content-free videos was rampant, even with companies that produced excellent videos. We would say about one-third of the companies completely avoided this problem while the rest had mixed issues with producing valuable non-self-indulgent videos.

Difficulty:

Impact:

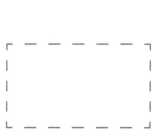

PUT VIDEO ON WEBSITE LANDING PAGES

An opening video on the front page of the company website will deliver a more detailed message that simply can't be conveyed with just a headline.

OPPORTUNITY

What is it you want your audience to know the moment they come to your site? What could you show in just 30 seconds that would get them to say, "That's exactly what I need!?"

DESIGN CONSIDERATIONS

- One option is an autoplay video with no sound (can be turned on by user) that has animated text or captions.

- Use one of the aforementioned interactive video tools (opportunity 42) that can track individual usage. Create a low-barrier offer to capture information from the visitor as they're watching the video.

CURRENT TREND

Forty percent of the company homepages we looked at had no video on the front page. Others that tried video on their site either buried it; made it not nearly as prominent; were inappropriately too long; or worse, provided a bad user experience that took visitors to another page where the video played in a tiny window. Conversely, ten percent of the companies impressed us with their front page video presentation.

Difficulty: ▮▮▮▮▮▮▮▮▯

Impact: ▮▮▮▮▮▮▮▮▮

48

TALK DIRECTLY TO THE VIEWER

Given that YouTube and many other social platforms invite response from the viewer, it's perfectly OK to create videos where the host looks directly into the lens and talks to the viewer.

OPPORTUNITY

If you're looking to inject humanity and/or humor in your videos, this is one of the simplest and most straightforward ways to do it. Best use cases for first-person videos are employer branding videos where your staff explains their job.

CONSIDERATIONS

- If you want to talk directly to the viewer you have to look directly into the lens, not slightly off to the side at a script, or at yourself as if you're shooting a selfie video. Look directly into the lens. Anything slightly off and you look untrustworthy.

- These types of videos are very much personality driven. Who in your office has that personality and on-camera presence to pull off this kind of video?

- First-person videos also do well as customer service videos.

CURRENT TREND

About 46 percent of the companies we looked at did little-to-no first-person videos. We were, though, really impressed with 12 percent of the companies who used the first-person video format to really connect with their audience. One CEO was a complete ham and really enjoyed making videos where he talked directly into the camera.

Difficulty:

Impact:

POST VIDEOS NATIVELY TO FACEBOOK AND LINKEDIN FOR SERENDIPITOUS VIEWING

While YouTube videos dominate in search, Facebook videos dominate social. Videos posted natively to Facebook offers another channel for serendipitous viewing through the News Feed. This is true with LinkedIn as well.

OPPORTUNITY

YouTube simply can't deliver serendipitous viewing like Facebook and LinkedIn can. Natively uploaded videos to Facebook autoplay in the News Feed and thus have 10 times higher reach than YouTube links on Facebook.[20] A video posted to Facebook will inevitably get more views in the first 48 hours the video is posted. But after that period of time, a Facebook video may never get another view. LinkedIn video lifespan appears to last as long as a week.

CONSIDERATIONS

- Facebook and LinkedIn both count a video being viewed is if it's seen for at least three seconds. YouTube is cagey about what it counts as a view, but it appears to be more than three seconds.

- A YouTube video will be seen by a user once they initiate some type of action such as search, discovery via social, being a subscriber, or seeing the video on a web page. Conversely, through autoplay, video discovery on Facebook and LinkedIn is unprompted, allowing for serendipitous discovery.

- Just because Facebook and LinkedIn views are often not initiated by the user, it doesn't mean they're not as valuable as a YouTube view. The value of a Facebook and LinkedIn video view is they're being seen by an audience that otherwise may never have a chance to see it.

- A YouTube video posted to Facebook will not autoplay like a video that's uploaded directly to Facebook.

- Some YouTube creators choose not to post on Facebook because they're trying to build and monetize a subscriber base. None of the businesses we looked at were trying to monetize their YouTube channel. They were purely looking for increased exposure.

CURRENT TREND

A whopping 40 percent of the companies we looked at had an either poor or non-existent video presence on Facebook.

While some companies looked at YouTube as a dumping ground for any produced video, it wasn't nearly as bad as what we saw on Facebook. Fortune 500 companies posted drastically off brand mobile phone videos with poor lighting and sound. Given that every company we looked at had many more Facebook followers than they had YouTube subscribers, it seemed like a missed opportunity to not crosspost their videos to Facebook.

Difficulty:

Impact:

MAKE FACEBOOK PLAYLISTS

Similar to YouTube, Facebook videos can also be organized into playlists.

OPPORTUNITY

Improve organization of your Facebook videos.

DESIGN CONSIDERATIONS

- A Facebook playlist appears to only provide better organization of Facebook videos. You can play all the videos, but it's unlikely people do that.

- Look at the tips for creative titling (opportunity 22) of YouTube playlists.

CURRENT TREND

A mere eight percent of companies took real advantage of the Facebook playlist feature. It appears no one knows that video playlists are even possible on Facebook.

Difficulty: ▮▮▮▮▯▯▯▯▯▯▯▯▯▯▯▯▯▯▯▯

Impact: ▮▮▮▮▯▯▯▯▯▯▯▯▯▯▯▯▯▯▯▯

51

ADD VIDEO TO YOUR FACEBOOK HEADER

The banner on your company Facebook page can be replaced with a short video.

OPPORTUNITY

At this point, so few companies are doing this that you can really stand out with a video playing in that top banner image.

DESIGN CONSIDERATIONS

- You'll want to create a video that plays well without sound.

- The banner video should deliver a clear message to what you're offering. It can be the same as the 30-second explainer video that you have on your website front page.

- Use your banner video to deliver the latest news about your company. Design a template that can easily be updated with information about products and events.

CURRENT TREND

Twelve percent of the companies did an excellent job adding eye-catching banner videos. About 3/4ths didn't bother adding an animated or video header.

Difficulty: ████████░░░░░░░░░░░

Impact: ████████░░░░░░░░░░░

52

USE BUGS FOR BRANDING

Like on network television, a continuous or periodic bug in the corner of a video offers a reminder as to who created the content.

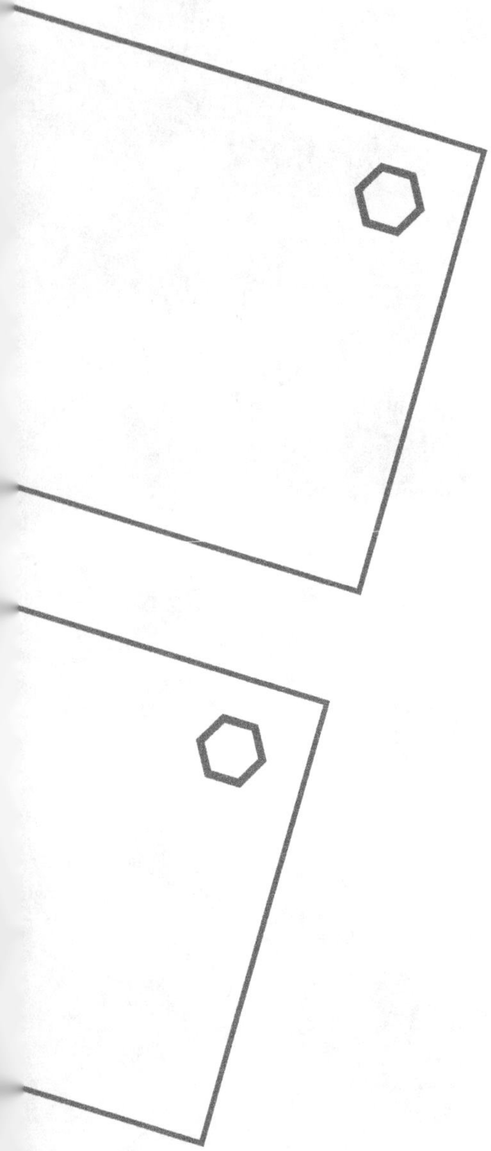

OPPORTUNITY

Beyond the obvious value of branding, a bug acts as a watermark preventing your material from easily being copied without attribution.

DESIGN CONSIDERATIONS

- If you do add a bug, avoid the lower right, the most common location, as that's where the YouTube subscribe button appears.
- If you're posting videos only on YouTube and you design a custom logo for the Subscribe button there's probably no need to add a bug.

CURRENT TREND

Eighty-two percent of the companies we looked at did not have a bug in their video. The other 18 percent only used the bug sporadically in a few videos.

Difficulty:

Impact:

53

INSERT LINKS TO VIDEOS IN YOUR EMAIL SIGNATURE

Anyone who receives an email from you is a natural audience for your videos.

OPPORTUNITY

Add a link to a video (within its playlist) in your email signature. Those emailing with you are an already connected audience.

DESIGN CONSIDERATIONS

- If you have an RSS feed for your videos, like in a blog, you can have a rotating billboard below your signature showing the latest videos.

- If you add a link to a YouTube video in an email that's read in Gmail, the thumbnail for the video will appear at the bottom of the email. If the reader clicks on that thumbnail, the video will play within their Gmail program.

CURRENT TREND

The resources to measure this are beyond the scope of this ebook.

Difficulty: �–ˆâ–ˆâ–ˆâ–ˆâ–ˆâ–ˆâ–‘â–‘â–‘â–‘â–‘â–‘â–‘â–‘â–‘â–‘â–‘â–‘â–‘â–‘

Impact: ▆▆▆▆▆▆▆▆▆▆▆▆▆░░░░░░░░

54

USE SUPPORTING ANIMATED TEXT

This is not the same thing as animated videos that tell their story only through animated text. Supporting animated text augments what's being said in the video. It's a more dynamic alternative to captions.

OPPORTUNITY

As mentioned before, videos with text or captions can extend viewing time by as much as 12 percent, according to Facebook. Unlike captions, animated text can be branded and offer a new layer of information.

DESIGN CONSIDERATIONS

- Plan ahead. When framing your shots, make room for animated text.

- If you're using animated text, it's best not to also add captions. Too much text on the screen, especially if it's similar, will confuse the viewer.

- Animated text can add contextual support to what's being said. It doesn't necessarily have to just repeat what's being said.

- By adding a new layer of information with animated text, you can often compress the time necessary to convey the information.

CURRENT TREND

Sixty percent of the companies we looked at didn't use animated text at all. But we did see about ten percent of the companies with some really impressive uses of animated text.

Difficulty:

Impact:

55

HAVE A VIDEO PRESENCE ON OTHER SOCIAL MEDIA PLATFORMS

Up until now the focus of video placement has been on YouTube, Facebook, or with a hosting platform that measures individual viewership. Videos can be distributed on other platforms such as Twitter, Instagram, and LinkedIn.

OPPORTUNITY

There's a huge audience of video viewers who don't subscribe to YouTube videos even though they watch videos online. You can extend the visibility of your videos by just placing them natively across multiple platforms.

DESIGN CONSIDERATIONS

- Not all video platforms should be treated the same. For example, if you'd like to distribute your video through Instagram it must be considerably shorter and ideally in a square format, not 16:9 format. Instagram will post the 16:9 format, but you'll get close to twice the real estate if you post in a square format.

- While you can upload videos to Twitter, it's not clear what the value is besides autoplay of the video.

- LinkedIn recently offered native videos, and like Facebook they autoplay and benefit from serendipitous discovery by your followers.

CURRENT TREND

While we didn't measure this, we do see more companies taking advantage of Instagram's video platform, especially with sponsored videos.

Difficulty:

Impact:

56

REACH YOUR AUDIENCE'S AUDIENCE ON LINKEDIN

Since the middle of 2017, LinkedIn has made it possible to upload videos natively to its platform.

OPPORTUNITY

As mentioned previously, native LinkedIn videos play within the user's feed. YouTube videos also autoplay on LinkedIn, but it appears LinkedIn gives preference to native videos.

LinkedIn also exposes your video to your second-degree connections at a much grander scale. This is evident from the traffic data provided by LinkedIn which appears to consistently show more traffic from second-degree connections than first-degree connections.

Unlike YouTube, which requires you to build an interested audience, your employees are probably already connected to a relevant industry audience on LinkedIn.

DESIGN CONSIDERATIONS

- If you're trying to get the most eyeballs on your video, you should upload all your corporate videos directly to LinkedIn.

- Most people follow individuals, not companies, on LinkedIn. For that matter, it's important to get your employees to share company videos on LinkedIn.

- LinkedIn currently has no management features, such as custom thumbnails and closed captions.

- Since the videos autoplay with no sound and there are no closed captions to add, make sure to add some animated text or open captions to the video so it makes sense without sound.

- LinkedIn provides spectacular tracking data of the companies, job titles, and locations of the people who watched your video. That data informs you as to what kind of audience your video attracts. Use this as a guide for future marketing and sales efforts.

CURRENT TREND

We waiting to measure this among the companies, since this feature is only a year old and it's being used minimally.

Difficulty:

Impact:

ENDNOTES

1   "The Top 500 sites on the web." *Alexa*. Amazon. 26 March 2018. Web. https://www.alexa.com/topsites

2   Ibid.

3   Robertson, Mark R. "YouTube search accounts for nearly 28% of all Google searches." *Tubularinsights*. 18 January 2010. Web. http://tubularinsights.com/youtube-search-december-2009

4   Kallas, Priit. "Top 10 Social Networking Sites by Market Share Statistics [November 2017]." *Dreamgrow*. 8 February 2018. Web. https://www.dreamgrow.com/top-10-social-networking-sites-market-share-of-visits

5   O'Neill, Megan. "The 2015 Video Marketing Cheat Sheet [Infographic]." *Animoto*. 7 May 2015. Web. https://animoto.com/blog/business/video-marketing-cheat-sheet-infographic

6   Hayes, Adam. "10 Video Marketing Statistics That Will Blow Your Mind." *Wyzowl*. 29 January 2018. Web. https://blog.wyzowl.com/10-video-marketing-statistics-that-will-blow-your-mind

7   Henry, Casey. "What Makes a Link Worthy Post - Part 1." *Moz*. 19 October 2009. Web. https://moz.com/blog/what-makes-a-link-worthy-post-part-1

8   Sruthi. "7 SEO facts of using video in landing pages to rank better in Google." *Animaker*. 28 November 2015. Web. https://blog.animaker.com/video-seo-facts-landing-pages

9   Ibid.

10   Fishman, Ezra. "Our Videos Dramatically Increased Our Visitors' Time on Page." *Wistia*. 16 December 2016. Web. https://wistia.com/blog/video-time-on-page

11   Moravick, Andrew. "Pardon the Disruption: The Impact of Video Marketing." *Vidyard and Aberdeen Group*. July 2015. Web. http://awesome.vidyard.com/rs/273-EQL-130/images/Vidyard_Aberdeen_Impact_of_Video_Marketing.pdf

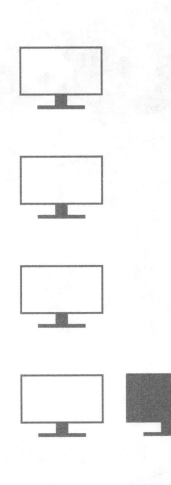

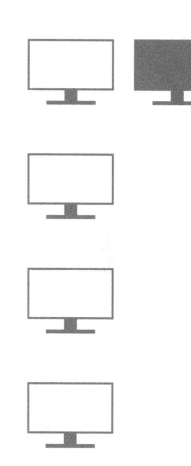

12   "Video SEO Cheat Sheet." *Digital Triggers*. https://s3.amazonaws.com/rvrb/Video-SEO-Cheat-Sheet.pdf

13   Moravick, *op cit.*

14   "Leading multimedia websites in the United States in November 2016, based on market share of visits." *Statista*. November 2016. Web. https://www.statista.com/statistics/266201/us-market-share-of-leading-internet-video-portals

15   Patel, Sahel. "85 percent of Facebook video is watched without sound." *Digiday*. 17 May 2016. Web. https://digiday.com/media/silent-world-facebook-video

16   Gesenhues, Amy. "Long-form video now makes up majority of time watched across all devices." *MarketingLand*. Third Door Media, Inc. 16 June 2017. Web. https://marketingland.com/long-form-video-content-hits-milestone-makes-majority-time-watched-across-devices-217667

17   "Facebook Videos Have a 10x Higher Viral Reach than YouTube Links." *Socialbakers*. 6 March 2013. Web. https://www.socialbakers.com/blog/1452-facebook-videos-have-a-10x-higher-viral-reach-than-youtube-links

18   "Video Marketing Statistics & Trends 2015." *Syndacast*. 31 July 2014. Web. http://syndacast.com/video-marketing-statistics-trends-2015

19   Cutler, Matt. "Why YouTube Viewers Have ADD and How to Stop It." *Ad Age*. 30 September 2010. Web. http://adage.com/article/digitalnext/marketing-online-video-viewers-quit-30-seconds/146218

20   Dean, Brian. "We Analyzed 1.3 Million YouTube Videos. Here's What We Learned About YouTube SEO." *Backlinko*. 28 February 2017. Web. https://backlinko.com/youtube-ranking-factors

METHODOLOGY

For the businesses we analyzed, we looked at tech companies that had significant video presences. We focused on many Fortune 500 tech companies, but also looked at medium-sized companies as well. With a few exceptions, all our companies posted at least 100 videos on YouTube and published their most recent video within the past year.

Much of our analysis was subjectively determined on a 1-5 scale. Given that consuming video requires significant time investment, often we made spot checks on a video without actually watching it all the way through.

DISCLAIMER

Although the information and data used in this report have been produced and processed from sources believed to be reliable, no warranty expressed or implied is made regarding the completeness, accuracy, adequacy, or use of the information. The authors and contributors of the information and data shall have no liability for errors or omissions contained herein or for interpretations thereof. Reference herein to any specific product or vendor by trade name, trademark, or otherwise does not constitute or imply its endorsement, recommendation, or favoring by the authors or contributors and shall not be used for advertising or product endorsement purposes. All trademarks are owned by their respective owners. The opinions expressed herein are subject to change without notice.

AUTHOR: DAVID SPARK

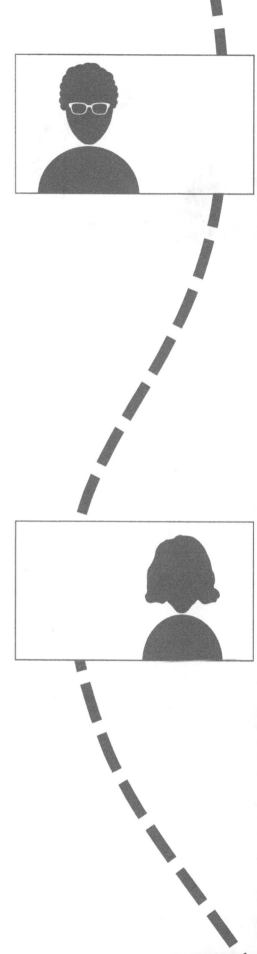

David Spark (@dspark) is a veteran tech journalist and founder of Spark Media Solutions.

Since 1996, Spark's work has appeared in more than 40 media outlets including eWEEK, Wired News, PCWorld, John C. Dvorak's "Cranky Geeks," and TechTV (formerly ZDTV). Spark also squandered more than a dozen years working as a touring standup comedian, a San Francisco tour guide, and comedy writer for The Second City in Chicago.

Today, Spark co-hosts the Tear Down Show and the CISO/Security Vendor Relationship Podcast, and blogs regularly on the Spark Minute. You can reach David at **david@sparkmediasolutions.com**.

Videos produced by Spark can be viewed at youtube.com/sparkmediasolutions and linkedin.com/in/davidspark

DESIGNER/ILLUSTRATOR: JOY POWERS

Joy Powers (@joypowers) is a multi-talented marketer with a passion for UI/UX, and has skills in art direction, design, animated video graphics, writing, editing, web development, and photography.

Powers is currently a partner with Spark Media Solutions, a B2B content marketing agency for the tech industry. She is responsible for creating the company's most popular content products and generating new revenue opportunities all while simultaneously cutting production costs by developing fast publishing techniques.

Prior to joining Spark Media Solutions, Powers served as the communications director for the Israeli Consulate in San Francisco. She also ran online marketing for the Jewish Community Federation in San Francisco.

joypowers.com

SPARK MEDIA SOLUTIONS

Founded in 2007, Spark Media Solutions is a B2B content marketing agency for the tech industry. The San Francisco Bay Area company uses media production to jump-start relationships for their clients.

Spark Media Solutions' products are designed to deliver clients' needs such as:

- Search and social visibility

- Thought leadership

- Influencer relations

- Lead generation and conversions

The content agency utilizes its decades of relations with the tech elite to produce videos, articles, images, and podcasts that are thoughtful, educational, funny, and entertaining. For more than 11 years, the company has worked with many well-known tech clients.

WORK WITH US!

Spark Media Solutions can provide the following media production, influencer, and consulting services, specifically for the B2B tech industry. Here are some suggestions on how to work with us:

Competitive analysis: Our research details, specifically on your competitors, will provide better insight into building your own video strategy.

Audit of your company's video presence: What video opportunities will give you the biggest bang for the buck? What are the simple opportunities you can take advantage of right now? What's necessary to stay competitive in your marketplace and how does your company stack up against the competition?

Content marketing that's relations-first focused: Traditional content marketing focuses on telling your story which may or may not be of interest to your audience. We found that a content marketing effort that focuses on your audience's interests first allows you to form relations. From there you can shift focus to brand-specific content marketing efforts.

Relation-based video production: With decades of experience working in the tech sector, our company goes beyond the traditional media production company. A combination of industry relations with entertaining, fun, and informative video production makes our firm the go-to choice for some of the best and biggest B2B tech companies.

Interested in working with us? Contact us at info@sparkmediasolutions.com.

FURTHER READING ABOUT VIDEO BY DAVID SPARK

How to Train Yourself to Create Great Videos

http://www.sparkminute.com/2013/11/25/how-to-train-yourself-to-create-great-videos/

Coolest Things You Can Learn from an Online Video

http://www.sparkminute.com/2013/02/21/coolest-things-you-can-learn-from-an-online-video/

How to Be Really Successful Producing a Crappy Video

http://www.sparkminute.com/2014/07/31/how-to-be-really-successful-producing-a-crappy-video/

Five Video Strategies that Are Totally Worth the Effort

http://www.sparkminute.com/2014/04/01/five-video-strategies-that-are-totally-worth-the-effort/

20 Great Ideas for Your Next Corporate Video

http://www.sparkmediasolutions.com/20-great-ideas-for-your-next-corporate-video/

21 Tips for Producing Funny "Man on the Street" Videos

http://www.sparkmediasolutions.com/21-tips-for-producing-funny-man-on-the-street-videos/

www.ingramcontent.com/pod-product-compliance
Lightning Source LLC
Chambersburg PA
CBHW080556060326
40689CB00021B/4874